Hi Bonnie,

Keep on

Rocking !

The 5 Best Decisions
THE BEATLES
Ever Made...

A HANDBOOK FOR
"TOP OF THE CHARTS"
SUCCESS

by
Bill Stainton

LITTLE CREEK PRESS

Seattle, WA

Raves for Bill's Keynote Presentation:

The 5 Best Decisions The Beatles Ever Made…and Why You Should Make Them Too!

"Bill Stainton was terrific—funny, interesting, and entertaining. He provided fun facts regarding the Beatles and application of their success for us to use now."
Barbara Hensley
Heller Ehrman White & McAuliffe

"Baby, you can drive my car…your presentation rocked. I wish you could have talked longer. Fascinating."
Nancy Kincl
Vulcan Capital

"Very motivational and encouraging. I found the information provided was relevant both personally and professionally. The information was delivered in a manner that kept it fun and interesting! Great presentation. The best this year!"
Rich Boswell
Raynier Institute & Foundation

"Not only does Bill know everything about the Beatles (we couldn't stump him…and we tried!), but he also knows how to translate their success to the world of business. It's a surprisingly good mix. The thought provoking business messages make his presentation valuable; the Beatles stories make it fun!"
Lauriann Reynolds
PEMCO Mutual Insurance

"An informative program that appeals to all ages and to any organization. Practical, yet entertaining. By far our best program of the year!

Ellen Callahan
Seattle Housing Authority

"Loved his presentation—it was so much more than I expected. I appreciated the fact that Bill included current information as well."

Margie Byrne
Federal Reserve Bank

"I really enjoyed Bill's presentation concerning the Beatles. It was informative and entertaining, with some hard-hitting realities on management and leadership qualities that makes it relevant to today's business climate. Since the presentation, I keep a copy of the "5 Decisions" on my desk.

Ronald S. Grasgreen
WestCoast Hotels

"It's interesting, intriguing, compelling, and engaging. You learn what the best in the business did…and how it also makes sense for your business. Plus, you'll learn all over again why you so enjoy hearing Twist and Shout!"

Brian Walter
The Effectiveness Institute

"Bill's extraordinary knowledge about the Beatles and his passion for this subject were evident, and he was able to convey his message in an entertaining and educational manner, with just the right amount of humor and audience participation."

Mary Rosen
International Association of Administrative Professionals

The 5 Best Decisions the Beatles Ever Made

Bill Stainton
Copyright © 2005

ISBN: 1-59872-114-3

Printed in the United States of America.

Published by:

Little Creek Press

Mukilteo, WA 98275

Ordering Information
To order more copies of this book please contact:

Little Creek Press
by calling:

888-5BEATLE

Also by Bill Stainton

Humor Us!
America's Funniest Humorists on the
Power of Laughter

Bombproofing:
How to Use Humor on the Platform
Without Falling on Your Face

ACKNOWLEDGMENTS

The great poet, John Donne, once wrote, "No man is an island." But then Simon & Garfunkle sang, "I am a rock, I am an island." So who knows? The point is, this book is not mine alone, and I owe a few debts of gratitude to some folks who, knowingly or unknowingly, helped me along the way:

My family, whose inquisitive minds and whose own books (much, *much* thicker than this) have been a constant inspiration throughout my life.

My friends at NSA, too numerous to name, who encouraged and/or shamed me into finally putting words to paper.

The late Bob Wooler, former DJ at the Cavern Club who introduced the Beatles 292 times, and who, over more pints of beer than I can count, shared many private Beatles stories...several of which he made me promise never to tell.

All the musicians I've played with over the years. From each of you I've learned something about music and life. And we did some good Beatles covers too!

And, of course, the Fab Four: the Beatles. Paul and Ringo, thanks for taking the time to chat. John and George, I'll catch you on the other side.

For all my audiences

who have been encouraging me to put this message into book form for many years.

CONTENTS

Introduction

February 9th, 1964. That was the day that I became a Beatles fan. I was six and a half years old, sound asleep in my bed, when my mom—in what was an unusually hip move for her—woke me up. Apparently, there was something on TV that she thought I might like to see. Something from England. Something called…the Beatles?

On that Sunday evening, I joined 73 million other Americans who were watching *The Ed Sullivan Show*. And, like many of them, I became a Beatles fan that day.

But Why a Business Book About The Beatles?

I'm not naïve (at least, that's what I naively tell myself). I realize that not everybody is a Beatles fan. My friend Chris, in fact, *hates* the Beatles! Does this make him wrong? Well, quite frankly…yes. But that may just be my bias showing. The fact remains, there are some people who just don't care for the

Beatles. They don't like the Beatles' music, their politics, their hair. Pick a reason.

The question of liking or not liking aside, let's also add the fact that the Beatles were together fewer than ten years, and then went through a very painful, protracted, and public break-up (this would later be called the "Jennifer Aniston model").

So, given all that, why on earth would I choose to write a business book based on the Beatles?

Simply because, despite their flaws, *the Beatles remain the gold standard when it comes to success.*

Why is it that any musical group of note invariably gets compared to the Beatles— and the Beatles invariably come out ahead?

It's because the Beatles *are* the gold standard. They define success in their industry (and their insights will help you do the same in yours!). In fact, they are *still*—decades after their break-up—a force to be reckoned with. If you want to know what a lasting success story is all about, think about this. For all intents and purposes, the Beatles broke up in 1969…

- In 2001, the biggest selling CD in America—for the year—was the Beatles' *1* CD.
- In 1995, in *Forbes* annual listing of the world's highest earning entertainers, the Beatles came in 3rd…after only Steven Spielberg and Oprah Winfrey.
- In 1996, they did the *very same thing again* (although Steven and Oprah changed places).
- In 2002, in a study by the *Sunday London Times* of British companies with the fastest-growing profits, the Beatles' company—Apple Corps.—came in first, with an annual growth rate of *194%*.

With that in mind, wouldn't you like *your* organization to be known as the "Beatles" of *your* industry? Clearly these four guys—John, Paul, George, and Ringo—did something right. Because results like these are not just a function of luck, or being at the right place at the right time. Results like these are the function of *decisions*— conscious decisions made over time that lead inevitably to the kind of success you and I would both like to achieve.

The rest of this book is about five of these decisions; what I call the Five Best Decisions The Beatles Ever Made. These decisions worked for the Beatles, and they will work for you. If you truly embrace these decisions, and make them your own, you'll be well on your way to enjoying the kind of success the Beatles have enjoyed ever since that historic night...February 9th, 1964.

The 5 Best Decisions THE BEATLES Ever Made...

SPREAD

THE

SPOTLIGHT

Decision #1:
Spread the Spotlight

"The fact is we were a team, despite everything that went on between us and around us."

- Paul McCartney

July 6, 1957. It's a warm Saturday afternoon in the seaport town of Liverpool, England. There's a neighborhood party going on (the "annual fete") at a church called St. Peter's, and at this party, a fledgling musical group is bravely plowing through their small repertoire. Their leader: a cocky, sarcastic—and on this particular day, somewhat drunk—16-year old named John Winston Lennon. And this was his band—The Quarrymen.

The Quarrymen played two sets that day: one in the afternoon, one in the evening. Among the audience members were two young boys, Ivan and James. During the break between sets, Ivan—who sometimes played tea-chest bass with The Quarrymen—introduced John Lennon to his 15-year old friend, James. James, who went by his middle name: Paul. Last name, McCartney. Perhaps you've heard of him.

July 6, 1957. The day John Lennon met Paul McCartney. And on that day, John Lennon had a decision to make. It would turn out to be the most important decision of his career.

See, Paul was a rock and roll fan himself, and he and John started talking about music. Pretty soon, the guitars came out. And John Lennon quickly found out that not only was this McCartney fellow better looking than he was, but he was also a better guitarist, *and*—at least at the time—a better singer. That's a triple-threat. And so 16-year old John Lennon had a decision to make.

And the decision was this:

"Do I keep the spotlight focused solely on me, as the star of The Quarrymen...or do I *spread the spotlight*, invite this McCartney fellow to join the group, and make the band better, make the *team* stronger?"

Let's put some perspective on this decision, shall we? If you're a man, I want you to think back to when you were sixteen years old. Are you there yet? Okay, as a sixteen year old adolescent, was there perhaps one single topic that seemed to consume *your entire brain, all the time?* (No, I'm not talking about sports.) And I mean your *entire* brain: the right half, the creative one, trying to imagine what it will be like when it happens; the left half, the logical one, trying to devise a way to *make* it happen in the first place!

By the way, for you women reading this—if you go back to when *you* were sixteen...I know *you* know what was on the guys' minds!

"A group becomes a team when each member is sure enough of himself and his contributions to praise the skill of others."

- Norman Shidle

Well, it turns out biology is no different on the other side of the Atlantic, and John Lennon was a healthy, red-blooded 16-year-old boy. Not only that, but he was the leader of his own rock and roll band. That's a pretty powerful combination! The last thing you want in this situation is competition. And so the *easy* decision—and the one that many of us probably would have made—would have been to put as much distance between ourselves and this McCartney triple-threat as possible.

But we all know what decision 16-year-old John Lennon made. And the day he made that decision, the Beatles were born. They wouldn't be *called* the Beatles for another few name changes and another few personnel changes, but that core team of Lennon and McCartney was born on that day in Liverpool. And all because 16-year old John Lennon made the decision to *spread the spotlight*.

"It's amazing what you can accomplish if you don't care who gets the credit."

- Harry S Truman

But I Don't *Want* to Spread the Spotlight

Oh, sure…you'll never say that *out loud*. But, from time to time, we all think it. There are times when we just don't want to spread the spotlight. There are times when we just don't want to share the credit. Times like:

- When we're trying to impress the boss
- When we're trying to impress a co-worker
- When we're trying to impress the cute new sales intern

For whatever reason, there are times when we like to keep the credit, the spotlight, all to ourselves. At these times, we should remember what former President Harry S Truman said:

> "It's amazing what you can accomplish *if you don't care who gets the credit.*"

Sure, we all have egos, and we all like to be recognized for our accomplishments. That's only human. But when we find ourselves *sabotaging our own long-term success* for the sake of a few short-term pats on the back, there's something wrong. In general, people work better, and produce better results, as a team.

Why do you think the songs of the Beatles are, generally speaking, better than the solo songs of Lennon and McCartney as individuals (there are exceptions, of course, but we're talking about a general body of work)? It's because John and Paul (and, to a lesser extent, George and Ringo), acting as a team, tended to "filter out" the excesses of each other. To use the vernacular, they cut out the crap. When the Beatles split up, and the four started their solo careers, there was no one there to cut out the crap. *Spreading the spotlight* works!

Two Sinister Syndromes

Have you ever suffered from "I can do it all myself" syndrome? Most of us have. Or its close cousin, "I can do it *better* by myself" syndrome? Granted, there are times when this may, in fact, be true. But most of the time it's just ego talking. We don't like to admit that we could use help. Sometimes, we're not secure enough with our own abilities or leadership to welcome somebody who may have a stronger skill set than we do. We think, consciously or not, that they might threaten our authority. We'll come up with other, more palatable, reasons of course; but at the core, it's a fear of losing control.

A true leader, however, knows that the surest way to achieve results is by building the best team possible, by not caring who gets the credit—in short, by spreading the spotlight.

> The essence of leadership is confidence.

Truth be told, we *can't* always do it all ourselves. Nor should we want to. Can you imagine the loss to the world (and not just the world of music) had John Lennon had either of these syndromes? So what might these syndromes be costing *your* organization?

A Very Simple Question

If you know somebody who doesn't seem to grasp this whole *spreading the spotlight* concept; who isn't terribly interested in sharing the credit; who's the poster child for "I can do it all myself" syndrome...then I encourage you to tell him or her the story of 16-year-old John Lennon. Because, ultimately, the question is a very simple one. When you think about yourself, and your relationship with your team, the question is a very simple one:

Would you rather be the *star* of the Quarrymen...or a *member* of the Beatles?

The 5 Best Decisions THE BEATLES Ever Made...

A SINGLE, SHARED VISION

Decision #2:
A Single, Shared Vision

"Where are we going, fellas?"
- John Lennon

When the Beatles were first starting out—well before they were even called the Beatles—there were over 300 other rock and roll bands. Not in the world. Not even in England. In Liverpool alone. Over 300 other rock and roll bands…and most of them were better than the Beatles.

So how did the Beatles manage to rise to the top? There were certainly a number of different elements, but the one that drove all the others was this one:

The Beatles had a *single, shared vision*.

A single, shared vision. And it was this: They were going to be bigger than Elvis!

Now, you have to understand something. Back in those heady days of the late 50s and early 60s, Elvis Presley was the biggest there was, the biggest there ever had been, the biggest there ever *would* be. And the Beatles were going to be bigger.

They knew *exactly* where they were going. As a matter of fact, whenever the band was feeling down—they didn't have any money, nobody would book them, they couldn't get a recording contract—*whenever* they were feeling down, their leader, John Lennon, would suddenly shout out, "Where are we going?"

And they'd all shout back, "To the top, Johnny!"

"Where's that, fellas?"

"To the toppermost of the poppermost!"

A little hokey? A little corny? Maybe. But the point is this: They all said the same thing. They all had that *single, shared vision*. And that, more than virtually anything else, is what drove them to the top. (Conversely, it was when they started to *lose* that single, shared vision that they began the internal descent that would eventually lead to their breakup.)

My Embarrassing Confession

Okay, it's "embarrassing confession" time.

From the age of sixteen to the age of eighteen, I was the drummer for the powerhouse, Top 40 rock and roll band…Liptastic.

Yes, you read that correctly. And the really sad thing is that it took us three days to come up with *that* name!

Liptastic was a powerhouse, Top 40 rock and roll band in my hometown of Lancaster, Pennsylvania. Home of the Pennsylvania Dutch.

The Amish.

Not exactly known for their rock and roll heritage. The point is that Lancaster, Pennsylvania was not what you might call a rock and roll "hotbed." There were not 300 other rock and roll bands in Lancaster. There were 20. And, of those 20, Liptastic was ranked 25th. We *never* thought we were going to be bigger than Elvis. Our *single, shared vision* was to play our set list as quickly as possible and go home. Not exactly a ticket to greatness.

But over in England, the Beatles *had* that single, shared vision. And it propelled them to the top of the charts.

Now, did having that single, shared vision, in and of itself, guarantee the Beatles' success? Of course not. It took luck, timing, talent—the alignment of a hundred different elements. But without having that single, shared vision *first*, none of the rest of it would have ever happened.

Keep it *Simple*

Now, the thing of it is, their vision—"bigger than Elvis"—is not a complicated one. They didn't bring in a team of consultants and run DISC assessments to come up with it. None of the four Beatles labeled it a "Mission Statement," framed it, and hung it in a lunchroom.

They *lived* it.

The point is, your single, shared vision doesn't have to be complicated. It doesn't have to be a paragraph long. It doesn't have to be printed on vellum in Olde English script.

What it *does* have to be…is simple.

Notice I said "simple," *not* "simplistic." "Bigger than Elvis" is simple. It's clear, it's understandable, and it doesn't require extensive memorization. And it drives *every* other decision. With *every* decision the Beatles made—what songs to record, what outfits to wear, what venues to play—the question, either conscious or subconscious, was, "Is this getting us closer to, or farther away from, our vision?"

Another Minor Success Story

Some years ago a fellow named Bill Gates had a company called Microsoft. He had a single, shared vision for his company, and it was this:

A computer on every desk.

Talk about simple! And that single, shared vision drove everything else that Bill Gates and Microsoft did. I understand it worked out pretty well for them.

The beauty of a simple vision is that it can be all encompassing. Something like, "Sell 42% more widgets this year" won't work. It's a fine *goal*, but a lousy *vision*. It can help you with widget decisions, but not much else. A simple, all encompassing vision, however, can drive an entire organization forward. It becomes a litmus test for everything else you do.

But, like a good goal, it must also be measurable. "Bigger than Elvis." "A computer on every desk." These are big statements; statements that inspire the emotions. That's vital. But they are also measurable. Again, "Is this decision getting us closer to, or farther away from, our single, shared vision?" When that vision is measurable, you'll always know.

What About You?

So what's *your* single, shared vision? What is it that will drive you, your team, and your organization to the "toppermost of the poppermost"?

What is it that will excite, inspire, and energize your team to reach that goal? What is it that will fire the emotions of everybody on your team?

Big questions? Yep. Difficult questions? You bet! Impossible questions? Not for the people who achieve unusual success.

So I want you to imagine that you're with your team right now. If you were to suddenly shout out, "Where are we going?" (and by the way, I don't suggest that you actually do this; your team will think that either, A: you've gone crazy, or worse, you've gone to a seminar)—would they all say the same thing? Do they have that *single, shared vision?*

When I ask that question during my keynote presentations, I'm always interested to see the response from the audience. Many people seem to take this question as a cue to look down at their feet. But the ones who are nodding "yes" are looking me right in the eye...and they're smiling. They're the ones who are well on their way to making that single, shared vision happen.

I've been in both places, and I can tell you from experience that it's more fun in the second group. And it all begins with a single, shared vision. What's yours?

The 5 Best Decisions
THE BEATLES
Ever Made...

PLAY TO YOUR
STRENGTHS

Decision #3:
Play to Your Strengths

"We'd be on the tour bus, and Roy Orbison was on the back of the bus, and he played us 'Pretty Woman,' and we'd think, 'We've gotta write one as good as that!' We were trying to improve all the time."

- Paul McCartney

The Beatles' first single was a song called *Love Me Do*. When it was originally released, it went to number seventeen in the British charts. That's a pretty respectable debut for a brand new band. But "respectable" doesn't get you to the "toppermost of the poppermost." It doesn't get you "bigger than Elvis."

The Beatles felt that they could do better.

And, more importantly (at least at this point), so did their producer, George Martin. Martin had been in the business a long time, and had a good set of ears. So when it came time for the Beatles to record their second single, Martin acquired for them a professionally written song called *How Do You Do It*. To his ears, this sounded like a hit record.

But when he offered it to the Beatles, they turned it down. They explained to Martin that they wanted all of their singles to be *Beatles originals*. (In those days, singles were the important recordings; albums were more of an afterthought.) In deference to their experienced producer, though, they *did* record a demo of the song. Martin then gave this demo to another band he was producing—Gerry and the Pacemakers—and told them to play it *just like the Beatles' version*. Gerry and the boys did just that…and their version went to number 1! It was a hit record—a sure thing—and the Beatles turned it down. Now, why would they do that?

They turned it down because of their third decision: the decision to *play to their strengths*. And to the Beatles, that meant their strengths as songwriters.

(Incidentally, the song the Beatles released instead of *How Do You Do It* was a John Lennon composition called *Please Please Me*. It went to number one in most of the British charts.)

The Beatles realized that if they were going to be true to their second decision—if they were really going to be "bigger than Elvis"—they couldn't be just another cookie-cutter band playing cookie-cutter songs. They had to answer a question that most of us never even ask:

"What is it that we can do better than anyone else?"

In other words, what is our biggest *strength?*

The Wrong Side of the Equation

So often, though, we focus on the other side of the equation. We tend to spend an inordinate amount of time focusing on our *weaknesses*. The dialog seems to be:

"My strengths will take care of themselves; I really don't need to worry about them. Instead, I'm going to spend the bulk of my time trying to improve my weaknesses, so that they, too, can become strengths."

It's a nice theory, but it usually doesn't work in the real world. What happens instead is that, while the weaknesses *do* improve a bit (although generally not to the level where we can honestly call them strengths), the strengths—because of lack of attention—tend to atrophy. And soon we find ourselves in this middle ground, which is called *average*.

A Telling Question

Not long ago, The Gallup Organization conducted a survey of nearly 200,000 employees in nearly 8,000 business units within 36 companies. Among other questions, the employees were asked this one:

At work, do you have the opportunity to do what you do best every day?

Before I give you the results of that survey, I want you to think about that question for yourself.

At work, do you have the opportunity to do *what you do best* every day?

If you're like 80 percent of the people surveyed, your answer is no. *80 percent!* What that means, of course, is that only *20 percent of employees feel they are "playing to their strengths" every day.*

What makes this particularly distressing is that those employees who *were* able to answer "yes" were more likely to:

- work in business units with lower employee turnover,
- work in more productive business units, and
- work in business units with higher customer satisfaction scores.

(Incidentally, Gallup has subsequently asked this question of more than 1.7 million employees in 101 companies from 63 countries—with the same results.)

The conclusion is clear: When we play to our strengths, we get better results!

A Faulty Assumption

Most organizations, though, take their employees' strengths for granted and focus instead on minimizing, i.e., fixing, their weaknesses. Now why, given the above research, would they do that? Marcus Buckingham, author of *First, Break All the Rules* and *Now, Discover Your Strengths*, believes it's because most organizations are built on a flawed assumption about people.

Most organizations, Buckingham says, operate on the assumption that a person's greatest room for growth is in his or her areas of greatest weakness. But the best organizations realize that just the opposite is true:

Our greatest room for growth is in the areas of our greatest strengths!

Strengths Within a Team

Look at your own team. Spend a few minutes and take a little "strengths inventory." What unique abilities do the individual members bring to the table? That's where your focus should be. Find ways to let them "play to their strengths" every day.

Within the Beatles, George Harrison was the lead guitarist. That's what he did best. The Beatles didn't waste a lot of time working with George on his weak drumming skills. Why? Because Ringo was already handling that job brilliantly. Drumming was what *he* did best. Each of the four Beatles *was* able to "play to their strengths"—every day.

What About You?

Since your strengths are unique to you, it's up to you to determine what they are. It's up to you to determine what it is that you do *best*…

- as an individual within a team
- as a team within an organization
- as an organization within an industry.

What is it that you can do *better than anyone else?* For the Beatles, the answer was songwriting. They poured the bulk of their energy into this strength.

Which is why the title of this book is *The 5 Best Decisions The Beatles Ever Made*, and not *The 5 Best Decisions Gerry and the Pacemakers Ever Made*.

The 5 Best Decisions
THE BEATLES
Ever Made...

CHALLENGE

THE

RULES

Decision #4:
Challenge the Rules

*"They'd say, 'Well, our rule book says...'
and we'd say, 'They're out of date, come
on, let's move!' We always wanted things
to be different because we knew that
people, generally, always want to move
on, and if we hadn't pushed them, the
guys would have stuck by their rule
books."*

- Paul McCartney

For the Beatles' fourth decision, I want to take you back to August 29, 1966. San Francisco. Candlestick Park. The Beatles are playing a concert in front of a sold out crowd of 25,000 screaming fans.

None of those fans knew it at the time—in fact, nobody except the four men on stage knew it—but it would be the last concert the Beatles would ever play.

And they were at the top of their game.

The top of their game, and they decided to call it quits. No more tours. No more concerts. No more live appearances. From that day on, the Beatles would become recording artists *only*.

And the rules said you couldn't do that.

The rules said you *had* to tour. You *had* to get out there with the people. You *had* to support your records with live appearances. To do otherwise was to commit career suicide. And that's what virtually everybody in the music business thought the Beatles had done by making the decision to stop touring.

Until June 1, 1967—nearly nine months to the day from that last show in San Francisco.

June 1, 1967. That's the day the Beatles released their new album—a monumental piece of work called *Sgt. Pepper's Lonely*

Hearts Club Band. This was an album that challenged virtually every rule in the book: musically, lyrically, visually. It's the album that turned rock and roll into an art form.

And it went to number one.

Without a tour.

See, for the Beatles, the "touring/concerts/live appearances" model no longer worked. They weren't enjoying it, and because the screaming of the fans kept them from actually hearing what they were playing, their musicianship was declining. More importantly, the music they were writing was getting more and more advanced—to the point that it would have been impossible, given the limitations of the day, to perform live.

In other words, "the rules" no longer supported the Beatles' vision. And so they challenged the rules.

By challenging the rules—by letting go of a system that no longer fit the vision—the

"*Rules are not
necessarily sacred.
Principles are.*"

- Franklin D.
Roosevelt

Beatles were able to take their career to a level that even they couldn't have dreamed of…a level of unsurpassed richness and creativity.

All because they decided to challenge the rules.

Yes, the Beatles could have kept on touring. They could have kept writing the same kinds of songs. They could have remained the "four moptops." It would have been easy for them to keep doing what they were already doing…and doing better than anybody else.

Two Traps

But when we keep doing what we've always been doing—even if we do it better than anyone else—we fall into two traps:

Trap #1: Complacency

When we keep doing something the same way, even if we're good at it (in fact, *especially* if we're good at it), we tend to get a bit complacent about it. We take it for

"If you obey all the rules, you miss all the fun!"

- Katharine Hepburn

granted. The excitement wears off, and we can find ourselves "phoning it in." The Beatles had already entered this stage, and they realized it. Thus, their decision to challenge the rules.

Trap #2: The Competition

Business is tough these days, and the competition can be fierce. If we keep doing things the same way, it makes it easier for the competition to catch up to us. And then, if we *keep* doing things the same way...the competition can pass us. By challenging the rules—by changing things up—we can go places the competition can't even imagine.

One of our finest philosophers, the late, great Katharine Hepburn, once said:

"If you obey all the rules, you miss all the fun!"

Hepburn certainly knew a thing or two about challenging the rules—and about having fun! And that brings up an important point:

Success should *be fun!*

Yes, by all means treat your success seriously. But "serious" doesn't mean "somber." The Beatles were *very* serious about their success…and they made sure to have fun along the way.

(Just one example: the last track on the *Sgt. Pepper's Lonely Hearts Club Band* album. Do you know what it is? Even people who are familiar with the album get this one wrong. They generally say *A Day In the Life*—which *is* the last *song*…but it's not the last *track*. The reason most people get this question wrong is because most people can't hear the last track—but their dogs can. That's because the last track on the *Sgt. Pepper's Lonely Hearts Club Band* album is a 15 kilocycle dog whistle that John Lennon recorded as a special message from himself to all the dogs in the world…just for fun!)

Legal Disclaimer

Please note, I'm saying *challenge* the rules. I'm not advocating that you go around *breaking* the rules willy-nilly. That's the kind of strategy that can get you ten to twenty in Leavenworth.

What I *am* advocating is that you give yourself permission to look closely at the way you are currently doing things and then ask some questions:

- *Why* am I doing it this way?
- Is there a different way to do this?
- Is there a *better* way to do this?

Give your teams permission to ask these same questions. Maybe there *is* a different way. Maybe there *is* a better way. Maybe you can make your *own* Sgt. Pepper.

The 5 Best Decisions THE BEATLES Ever Made...

DO WHAT IT TAKES

Decision #5:
Do What It Takes

"The reason we were twice as good as anyone else is because we worked twice as hard as anyone else."

- Paul McCartney

Okay, let's be honest here. You can *spread the spotlight* and have a great team; you can develop a *single, shared vision*; you can identify and *play to your strengths*; and you can even *challenge the rules*. But until somebody rolls up their sleeves and actually *does the work*, nothing is going to happen.

And that's what this final decision is all about: getting the work done...*doing what it takes*.

To illustrate what I mean, let's take a snapshot of the Beatles' career:

- 12 albums, 11 of which went to #1
- 22 singles, 17 of which went to #1
- 4 movies
- 52 BBC radio appearances
- over 1,400 live appearances

And they did virtually *all* of this…in just five years.

Five years! For most bands today, that would mean two albums and two tours.

Remember, the Beatles' first *Ed Sullivan* appearance was on February 9, 1964. The last time all four Beatles were in the studio together was August 20, 1969.

Now, I don't know what *you've* been doing for the past five years. *My* big accomplishment during that time span? I fixed my upstairs toilet. And when I say *I* fixed it, I mean I called a guy, and he came over and took care of the problem.

What did the Beatles do in five years? They did the Beatles.

A Lesson from Seinfeld

Before I became a keynote speaker, I was a television producer. In that capacity, I had the good fortune of working with Jerry Seinfeld several times. On one of these occasions, we were sitting together in the green room (which, like virtually all green rooms everywhere, was painted a drab beige). He told me a story about a moment that changed his career.

One day, while he was a struggling young comedian in New York, Jerry decided he didn't feel like spending the day writing jokes. It was a nice day, so he chose to take a walk instead. While on his walk, he happened to see a construction crew that was just finishing its lunch break. As the workers returned to the job, Jerry thought to himself:

"Those guys don't want to go back to work. I'm sure they'd rather be taking a walk themselves. But instead, they're going back to work, because that's their job...that's what they do."

And with that, Jerry Seinfeld went back to his apartment and spent the day writing jokes…because that was his job. Instead of taking the day off, he made the decision to *do what it takes*…and he told me that *that*, more than anything else, is what made the difference in his career.

The Other 20%

Woody Allen once said, "Eighty percent of success is showing up." Now, I'm a huge fan of Woody's…but with all due respect, that eighty percent will only get you so far. Gerry and the Pacemakers "showed up." They're not the Beatles. A thousand other software companies "showed up." They're not Microsoft.

Yes, showing up will get you in the game. You may even stick around for a few innings. But the people who *win* the game—the ones who become legends—are the ones who target the other twenty percent.

Not the Bare Minimum

So when I say *doing what it takes*, I mean *doing what it takes to achieve the success you want in life*. I *don't* mean just doing what it takes to get by. If that's all you do, that's all you'll get.

See, there's a principle that the universe operates on. It's a principle Jerry Seinfeld understood; it's a principle the Beatles understood. And the principle is this:

To a large degree, the results you get out of life will be equal to the effort you put in.

That's important, so I'm going to repeat it.

To a large degree, the results you get out of life will be equal to the effort you put in.

Re-read the quote from Paul McCartney that started this chapter. It's a perfect example of this principle in action.

Now, having said all of the above, I'm pretty sure that you already know, and practice, this principle. Why do I assume this? Because you're reading this book. That tells me that you've probably already achieved a certain level of success, and you're ready to take that success to the next stage. You're ready to go to the "top of the charts."

People who don't "get" this principle don't read books like this. They're the ones who refuse to work harder because they're "not getting paid enough." They operate on the principle that things would get better if they could just "catch a break."

They don't understand that their rewards will equal their effort, that they get out of life what they put into it, and that if they want to get more...they have to give more.

In short, they don't understand what you understand, and what the Beatles understood. In fact, the Beatles may have put it best...and I'm going to end with this, because the Beatles ended with this...

The 5 Best Decisions

THE BEATLES

Ever Made...

AND IN

THE END...

And in the end...

"Life is cause and effect. What you get is the effect; what you give is the cause."
-   Bill Stainton

The last album the four Beatles released together was *Let It Be*. But the last album the four Beatles actually *recorded* together was *Abbey Road*. *Abbey Road* was the last music the four Beatles ever made together. And, *as they originally designed it*, the last words of the last song of the last Beatles album were these:

And in the end...the love you take...
is equal to the love you make.

Folks, that's not a bad way to go out. It's a pretty good way to cap off the most significant career in pop music history. But what does it mean...really?

Well, if you look at it in a broader sense, it means exactly what we've just been talking about. It means that, in the end, you get out of life what you put into it.

You probably know people who say things like, "I'd work harder if they'd pay me more money," or, in its more common iteration, "I'm not getting paid enough to work this hard." These people are getting the equation backwards. They haven't figured it out yet. They don't realize that this is the equivalent of looking at a bare patch of earth and saying, "If you give me flowers, I'll give you water and fertilizer."

And in the end, the love you take is equal to the love you make.

It means: If you want to get more, you have to give more. And the giving comes first.

So no more whining, no more griping, no more complaining. No more excuses. They won't work. What *will* work? The 5 Decisions we've talked about in this book:

1. *Spread the Spotlight:* Put together the strongest team you can, and be willing to share the credit.

2. *A Single, Shared Vision:* Define what it is that will emotionally (yet measurably) drive you and your team to your ultimate destination.

3. *Play to Your Strengths:* Discover and focus on the individual strengths of each of your team members. Decide what it is you do best...as an individual, as a team, and as an organization.

4. *Challenge the Rules:* Ask questions like, "Is there a different way to do what I'm doing?" "Is there a *better* way?" (And don't forget to have fun!)

5. *Do What It Takes:* Decide where you want to go. Obtain the tools you'll need to get there. Put in the time. In virtually all cases, your rewards will equal your effort.

You get out of life what you put into it.

So, if you want to get more:

- in your career
- in your community
- in your relationships

...you have to give more.

Because, in the end, the love you take *is* equal to the love you make.

Bill's Top 10 Beatles Books

1. Philip Norman, **Shout!: The Beatles in Their Generation,** Fireside Books

2. The Beatles, **The Beatles Anthology,** Chronicle Books

3. Mark Lewisohn, **The Complete Beatles Chronicle,** Hamlyn Books

4. Mark Lewisohn, **The Complete Beatles Recording Sessions,** Three Rivers Press

5. Hunter Davies, **The Beatles,** W. W. Norton & Company

6. Tim Riley, **Tell Me Why: The Beatles: Album by Album,** Da Capo Press

7. Andy Babiuk, **Beatles Gear,** Backbeat Books

8. Larry Kane, **Ticket to Ride,** Running Press Book Publishers

9. Nicholas Schaffner, **Beatles Forever,** McGraw-Hill

10. Mark Hertsgaard, **A Day in the Life: The Music and Artistry of the Beatles,** Delta

10 Things You Probably Didn't Know About The Beatles

1. John Lennon and Paul McCartney once booked themselves as a duo called The Nerk Twins.

2. The harmonica John plays on *Love Me Do* was shoplifted from a store in Holland.

3. The refrain of "very strange" in the song *Penny Lane* is an inside joke; there was a father-son law office there called "Strange & Strange."

4. The Beatles once lost a talent competition to a woman who played the spoons.

5. One female fan trying to get backstage at a Seattle Beatles concert fell 25 feet down a ventilation duct and landed at Ringo's feet.

6. The Beatles were the first rock and roll band to play Carnegie Hall, but Carnegie Hall thought they were getting a classical group, as the Beatles had been booked as "a British quartet."

7. The Beatles and the Rolling Stones had a tacit agreement not to release their recordings at the same time.

8. Erich Segal, the author of *Love Story*, was one of the writers for the Beatles' film, *Yellow Submarine*.

9. The original title for the *Rubber Soul* album was *The Magic Circle*.

10. John's song, *Good Morning, Good Morning*, was inspired by a corn flake commercial.

About the Author

Bill Stainton

Bill is a multiple Emmy Award winning TV producer, performer, and writer; a popular keynote speaker; and an internationally-recognized Beatles expert.

Not bad for a kid who grew up behind a dairy farm in the Amish countryside of Lancaster, Pennsylvania.

The owner of two businesses, and a 20+-year veteran of corporate management, Bill is also the author of nine corporate training programs which are distributed worldwide.

As a keynote speaker (and former president of the Northwest chapter of the National Speakers Association), Bill has entertained and enlightened thousands with his Customized Humorous Keynotes, as well as his popular programs on humor, creativity…and, of course, *The 5 Best Decisions the Beatles Ever Made!*

Ovation Consulting Group, Inc.
4522 131st Place SW
Mukilteo, WA 98275
425-741-3972 • 888-5BEATLE
Fax: 425-742-2881